Charles Townshend

# A Letter to the Right Honourable Charles Townshend

Charles Townshend

**A Letter to the Right Honourable Charles Townshend**

ISBN/EAN: 9783337195809

Printed in Europe, USA, Canada, Australia, Japan

Cover: Foto ©ninafisch / pixelio.de

More available books at **www.hansebooks.com**

# LETTER

TO THE RIGHT HONOURABLE

# CHARLES TOWNSHEND.

*Quid enim necesse est convocari Tribus,*
*Contrarie Populum si idem effici jure vetere,*
*Et jam olim constituto Potest?*

QUINTILIAN.

---

LONDON:

Printed for W. NICOLL, in St. Paul's Church-Yard. MDCCLXIV.

[ Price One Shilling. ]

# A
# LETTER
## TO THE RIGHT HONOURABLE
# CHARLES TOWNSHEND.

IF it is poſſible that the Defence of the Minority can be indeed the production of that name which has been ſo often quoted, in order to give it that weight from authority which it could not derive from it's argument, neither the public nor yourſelf will have reaſon to be ſurpriſed at this addreſs to you.

SURFEITED as the Town was by that groſs and heavy food, with which they had been crammed in Budgets, Letters to the Cocoa-Tree, *&c.* it could not but be pleaſed with the expectation of ſomething more *piquant*, in a diſh which they were told was ſeaſoned and ſerved up to them by the *Clouet* of the party. ----- To ſpeak without a metaphor, it was expected from you, Sir, that the counſels and purpoſes of that Party, to which you had lent your name, ſhould be ſtated with preciſion, and defended with ability: That a queſtion, which the publication of the numbers on each ſide had inclined many to think was of a very intricate and doubtful nature, ſhould have been, by you, proved as eſſential to the liberties of the ſubject, as it had been repreſented.

How theſe well-grounded expectations have been anſwered, this Letter ſubmits to your conſideration. And let me be allowed to expreſs the ſame degree of *attachment to the reputation and merit of Two hundred and thirty-four*, which you have ſhewn to thoſe of *Two hundred and twenty*; with this additional plea in my favour, That however high the reputation of the Minority may be in your or their own opinion, yet, while they continue to bear that name, they are private men, of whoſe opinions and conduct we may think even with contempt, with-

out

out infringing any conſtitutional law: And that it is the condemnation of the *Majority* in parliament, *which ſacrifices the fair report of the proceedings of the Commons of England, and Truth itſelf.* How far ſuch a condemnation is in itſelf conſtitutional, or how far the endeavouring to leſſen the weight of their deciſions in the minds of the People, and to alienate from Parliament the affections of their conſtituents, is wiſe, I would recommend it to you to conſider.

BEFORE I proceed to the main purpoſe of this letter, I cannot help congratulating myſelf upon one advantage which attends me. For while *you*, Sir, were obliged to give an importance to your Adverſary, by raiſing him from the ſituation of an humble writer in the Gazetteer to *miniſterial authority*, and dignifying his Paper with the title of *Favourite Proclamation of the Miniſtry*; I am ſure of enobling my thoughts, by taking for the ſubject of them *your* opinions and reaſonings. Every thing which relates to theſe will be thought important by the Public.

WITHOUT enquiring whether you have any better foundation for the consequence you have bestowed on the Gazetteer, than the other writers of your Minority have had for giving constantly to the Ministry such arguments as they could easily confute, and such measures as they knew the Public would condemn ; I shall apply myself to the examination of your Answer to it. ------ To do this it will, I think, be clearer to state separately the points in debate, and the arguments upon each of them, than to follow, page by page, the progress of the Defence. It will at least have for me this advantage, That my composition and language will not be brought into the Reader's eye at the same time with that of the *Defence*. And I know you and myself too well to avoid a comparison on these subjects. It is my *Cause* alone which I think superior.

THE chief points stated in your Pamphlet, and upon which the whole Defence depends, are divided into Legal and Parliamentary.

WITH respect to the first, I must confess that I enter upon this part of the subject with all the apprehensions which your character may naturally be supposed to create: And you are become the more formidable to me in this respect, from having joined a *legal* education to a very lively and accurate understanding. I proceed to consider the manner in which you have employed these advantages.

YOUR positions are, page 8th, *That the question of the legality of the warrant is not now* sub judice, *nor has ever yet been in a course of legal determination;* and that the delay of bringing it into issue is to be charged on those who granted, and who acted under it. To prove this, you say you will state fairly and precisely the nature of the several bills of exceptions. You quote the bill in the case of Wilkes against Wood, and would be understood to give the substance of it: And as, in your transcript, there is no mention of the legality of the warrant, you conclude that it was not then in issue. I would gladly ask you, How you can take upon you to assert what is contained in the bill of exceptions,

exceptions, which has never yet been made public? As therefore I pretend to no other information than what is of public notoriety, I ſhall leave you to triumph on this part of the argument, till the detection of it's fallacy, of which I have no manner of doubt, can be made appear from free and open recourſe to the original, or at leaſt authenticated copies of the bill.

It would be a ſufficient anſwer to your reaſoning, to remind you, That any point of a bill of exceptions may be brought in iſſue immediately: And therefore, to ſay that this has never yet been in a courſe of legal determination, is not to ſpeak preciſely. But I will advance a ſtep further, and prove to you, that the matter has not only been in iſſue, but decided as far as the opinion of *one* Chief-Juſtice can determine it. It is true that it was not upon the illegality of the warrant that the Jury found in Leach's caſe: It is no leſs true, that the Chief-Juſtice declared it illegal in that caſe; and, in the caſe of Wood, both judge and jury *determined* it to be ſo.

Mr. Wood had pleaded the warrant in juſtification; and which, had it been allowed legal, would have juſtified him againſt the action of treſpaſs. When, therefore, the jury gave damages, they concurred with the opinion of the Chief-juſtice in declaring the warrant illegal. If, however, this determination ſhould not be thought concluſive till affirmed by the other ſuperior courts; let me remind you that it is *ſub judice*, and muſt come in queſtion on the Writ of Error, Wood at the ſuit of Wilkes. ----- It is equally *ſub judice* in the cauſe of Leach.

How ſoon the expectations of the Public may be ſatisfied, and this cauſe, ſo important to liberty, judicially and finally determined, you are more likely to learn than I am: For you are miſinformed, if you believe that the delay in theſe cauſes proceeds from the parties *accuſed*. Had a ſpeedy iſſue been really the wiſh of thoſe who affect ſo much earneſtneſs for it, the way to obtain it was obvious. They had only to have demurred to the legality of the warrant, in any of thoſe cauſes wherein it was pleaded as a juſtifica-

juſtification; and the demurrer would immediately have been tried.

BEFORE I quit this part of the ſubject, I cannot avoid taking notice of a ſingular aſſertion in the 21ſt page of the Defence: *Should a Secretary of State, upon intelligence of any crime really formidable to the common-wealth, and of a nature requiring diſpatch and ſecreſy, be under a neceſſity of iſſuing ſuch a warrant as is now complained of; and ſhould his meſſengers, in purſuit of the offenders, take up an innocent man; is it reaſonable to ſuppoſe, that any jury would be found ſo narrow in their notions of government, as not to attend to a diſtinction, clearly made and well ſupported, upon the peculiar circumſtances of ſuch a criſis? Or, ſhould prejudice or ignorance influence the determination of juries, would not the officers thus ſuffering for the public, be relieved by the interpoſition of parliament?*

NOT the caſe which you here ſuppoſe, but a caſe much ſtronger, has actually exiſted. A libel was publiſhed, and continuing to be diſperſed, tending to raiſe traiterous inſurrections. You will not deny this to be a crime really formidable to the common-wealth, and of a nature requiring dispatch and secrecy. Upon *your* principles, therefore, the Secretary issued the warrant. His messengers, in the execution of it, took up not an *innocent* man, but the *guilty* Author; and yet the jury were so far from acting upon the principles you give to them, that they have given damages. And you yourself are so far from *wishing* the interposition of parliament, to *relieve* the officers thus suffering for the public, that you *sollicit* it, to give still greater edge to the like verdicts of juries.

UPON the parliamentary part of your argument, your assertions are these: That the question concerning the illegality of *certain general warrants was a particular, not a general question: That, in imitation of former proceedings of parliament*, (which you have quoted in your Pamphlet) *they meant to confine themselves to the single case before them: That it was taken up by the Minority entirely unconnected with the case of Mr. Wilkes; and that it was not an inconsistent conduct, in those who voted for the motion, to reject the remedy of a bill.* Upon the first of these points, you have ſaid, page 5, That you think it might be juſtifiable, in conſideration of the public danger, the nature of the offence, *&c.* to *connive* at the uſe of general warrants of apprehenſion; but that, in the caſe of a libel already publiſhed, this power is neither neceſſary nor expedient to be lodged in any hands: That the Minority ſaw this diſtinction, adopted it; and that, therefore, they framed their motion from the caſe before them, and confined it to a ſeditious libel.

Let me now offer to you my reaſons, for aſſerting that the queſtion was underſtood to be *general*, not *particular;* and that the Minority did not even ſee the diſtinction which you ſay they adopted. I muſt recal that hour to your recollection, and I doubt not it will give you pleaſure, when the Minority were held out to the Public as champions of their freedom; and we were taught to expect, from the hands of thoſe confederate Chiefs, that great ſupplement to Magna Charta, the Deliverance *from all general warrants.* It was by this promiſe, and by this

this alone, that they trusted they should unite to them the wishes and assistance of the people. And this was the sole foundation of the claim which they so boldly asserted, to the Title of *Defenders of the Freedom and Constitution of Great Britain*. The writers of their party took immediately the same tone. I have found the pamphlets of two of them, and I will quote to you their words, to prove that their common creed is contrary to the sentiments which you have lately given them; and by which you, who are less orthodox and more refined, have endeavoured to palliate the absurdities of the Party Faith.

THUS the author of the Letter to the Cocoa-Tree, page 15. "One would be
" apt to think some extraordinary pru-
" dence in those who have ventured
" to execute general warrants, and an
" uncommon terror in the poor and
" helpless persons, who have hereto-
" fore been oppressed by the tyranny
" of them, had hitherto kept them
" concealed from public view, that
" they have not before now felt the
" indignation of the courts of law.

"Even thoſe who have not the advan-
"tage of the ſcience of the law, could
"not but perceive, at firſt ſight, how
"inconſiſtent general warrants were
"with the conſtitution." And again,
page 17, "The object in view was not
"barely to condemn general warrants
"without name.----Depriving the ſub-
"ject of his liberty, without a charge
"upon oath, *or ſomething as ſtrong, is e-
"qually illegal. Cloſe confinement for a bailable
"offence, arbitrary evaſions of the* Habeas
"Corpus, *and, above all, the unwarrantable
"ſeiſure of papers, were objects highly wor-
"thy the weightieſt interpoſition."* Where
you ſee that the avowed Defender of
the Party, collecting, with indefatiga-
ble induſtry, every cauſe of complaint
againſt the warrant iſſued by Lord
Hallifax, has introduced all thoſe circumſtances, which are now confeſſed-
ly waved, and omitted that which you
have ſtated as the only ground upon
which the motion of the Minority was
founded; namely, That the particular
caſe did not call for it.

Thus alſo, in that affectionate Defence of Mr. Conway, called the Coun-
ter-Addreſs, it is ſaid, page 15, "The
"voice

" voice of the nation went along with " the conduct of Mr. Conway. They " were, and are still of opinion, that " general warrants are radically and " alarmingly dangerous to liberty." This language, you will allow to be very different from yours: And you will not, it is probable, deny that the Author of it was more conversant with the party than yourself. Nor were these sentiments confined to the Minority-agents *without* doors; their most professed leaders held exactly the same language. That it is either decent or proper to repeat the expressions made use of in Debates, the example of the Defence has not yet convinced me.

Without quoting, therefore, the particular words, I am at liberty to ask you, whether you do not recollect some violent, though lively declamations against general warrants, and the encroaching powers of Office? Was not the insecurity of *every* subject pathetically lamented, while such warrants were allowed as might be employed against *any?* You must remember, that the whole fire of oratory was directed

directed againſt the, as it was called, *unconſtitutional power*, not againſt that particular exertion of it, which they who moved the queſtion had formally deſired might be conſidered as without the reach of the propoſed reſolution; and ſtill leſs avowedly was it uſed, to prove that *a falſe, ſcandalous, and ſeditious libel, tending to excite the people to traiterous inſurrections*, had not called for, and did not warrant the interpoſition of the Secretary of State, by ſuch warrant as was the moſt ordinary and effectual remedy.

ANOTHER proof to me, is the number of the Minority in that day. The queſtion, as the terms of it are now ſtated by you, was whether Mr. Wilkes's caſe was ſuch a one as, *in conſideration of the public danger, and the nature of the offence*, juſtified the uſe of a general warrant. But I will venture to appeal to your own opinion, whether, if this had been generally underſtood to be the real ſtate of the queſtion, the Minority would have been ſo numerous, as to have deceived even your penetration into an opinion of their ſucceſs. Would ſo large a body, think

you,

you, have taken upon themſelves to avow, or will they feel themſelves indebted to you for giving them the opinion, that a ſeditious libel, *tending to excite traiterous inſurrections againſt his Majeſty's government*, circulated with diligence in the Weſtern counties, where it might do moſt miſchief, ſhould have been left to ſcatter it's poiſon, and wait for it's puniſhment, till the ſlow forms of the courts of law had been gone through?

THE diviſion, which was ſo numerous as to induce you to pronounce the Adminiſtration *vanquiſhed in that day*, was, you muſt remember, owing to the great and ſucceſsful pains which were taken to *prevent* the *caſe of Mr. Wilkes from appearing the cauſe of oppoſition*. Though you have now more honeſtly confeſſed, by declaring the motion to have been formed upon Mr. Wilkes's caſe only, that they are one and the ſame.

THE laſt reaſon that I have for thinking that the motion was general, is drawn from the terms in which it is conceived. If I had diſputation in view more than truth, I ſhould have a right to inſiſt, that it was not poſſible for you to think that a motion, which declared general warrants, in the caſe of *ſeditious libels only*, illegal, could extend to the caſe of the Publiſher of a libel, *tending to raiſe traiterous inſurrections.* The nature of theſe libels is ſo exceedingly diſtinct, the criminalty of the latter ſo much greater, and it's conſequences ſo much more dangerous than thoſe of the former; that, if the motion had paſſed in the words which you have ſtated, it could not have even appeared to comprehend the warrants iſſued by Lord Halifax. Nor will I detain you with any remarks on the extraordinary accuracy and preciſion, which you was ſo apprehenſive of failing in. The political legerdemain of ſubſtituting the queſtion moved on the 14th, for that which was really debated on the 17th of February, carried it's reaſons with it ſo obviouſly, that the diſcovering the fineſſe is ſufficient, without further animadverſion. If one might be at liberty to wiſh upon this ſubject, it ſhould be, That the fact had been well eſtabliſhed, before you had called thoſe who miſtake it contemptible for ignorance, or chargeable with falſehood. But, waving theſe advantages, it is impoſſible not to ſee that the motion really debated, though brought nearer to the caſe of Mr. Wilkes, was not ſo preciſe as to include it, much leſs to be confined to it.

To prove this you will obſerve, that, if the motion had paſſed, not only every other ſpecies of general warrants would have received countenance upon that old maxim, *exceptio affirmat regulam*; but a ſecretary of ſtate would ſtill have remained at liberty to iſſue a general warrant for apprehending the author, printer, or publiſher of any libel, which tended to raiſe traiterous inſurrections. For the reſolution of the Houſe of Commons could not have comprehended this caſe, as not containing the words which deſcribed it. And yet you have aſſerted, that, upon this ſingle caſe, the motion was formed. If that had been true, and the Minority had meant to avow that Mr. Wilkes's intentions of raiſing traiterous inſurrections ſhould not have been prevented by a general warrant; their motion would have contained the words in which the parliament had defcribed his paper on the 19th of January: And it would have ftood thus, "Refolved, *that a general warrant for ap-* "*prehending the authors*, printers, and "publifhers of a falfe, fcandalous, "and feditious libel, containing ex- "preffions of the moft unexampled "infolence and contumely towards "his Majefty, the groffeft afperfions "upon both Houfes of Parliament, "and the moft audacious defiance of "the authority of the whole legifla- "ture; and moft manifeftly tending "to alienate the affections of the peo- "ple from his Majefty, to withdraw "them from their obedience to the "laws of the realm, and to excite "them to traiterous infurrections "againft his Majefty's government, "is not warranted by law; although, "*&c.*"

BUT whatever were the *concealed* de- figns of the Minority, and however poffible it might have been to procure a gentleman to move a refolution thus worded; it is probable that it would have

have had the ill fortune to make little impreſſion on the body of the Houſe: And though it might be neceſſary for the purpoſes of faction, and to give to the Minority a poſſibility of conqueſt, that ſuch words ſhould be uſed as would be known to be intended againſt Lord Halifax by thoſe who were in the ſecret, (and the word *treaſonable* was made choice of for that purpoſe;) yet had the motion been formed in the words of the reſolution juſt now quoted, deſcribing Mr. Wilkes's caſe, it would never have influenced thoſe who, on that day, joined you upon the footing of defending a general maxim; and who would not have contributed their aſſiſtance to a direct attack on Lord Halifax, for exerting his authority in an inſtance which they thought fully juſtified it's interpoſition. Had the Minority indeed confined themſelves to the caſe before them, you would have had reaſon for your aſſertion, that their conduct was juſtified by it's imitation of former parliaments. For, of the inſtances you have produced, there is not one but what is tied down to the ſingle caſe before them. I will take them as they are ſtated in the Defence.

THE reſolution paſſed by the Houſe of Commons againſt Lord Nottingham was, that the taking Lord Danby by *that warrant* was illegal. In the caſe of Lord Chief-Juſtice Scroggs, the Houſe acted upon the ſame principles, and reſolved that the *ſaid warrants*, (namely thoſe which had formed the ſubſtance of the charge againſt him) were arbitrary, and illegal. The reſolution paſſed in the caſe of Lord Chief-Juſtice Keeling is equally preciſe: The words of it are, "That the "precedents and practice of fining ju-"ries is illegal;" referring evidently to thoſe precedents, and that practice, which had been the object of enquiry at their bar. Had they meant to have trod in the ſteps of former parliaments, the way was open to them.

THERE were indeed two methods of proceeding; the one ſo ſpecial and preciſe, as to have decided upon, and condemned the warrant iſſued againſt Mr. Wilkes: The other ſo general, as to to have indeed ſecured the liberty of the ſubject, if it had been their intention, and had ſtood in need of their interpoſition. The objection to the former was, the character of the perſon in whoſe defence the motion muſt have been made, and of whom it muſt have diſcovered them to be the friends and protectors. The latter would not have anſwered their chief purpoſe, an oblique cenſure on individuals.

I WOULD juſt obſerve, by the way, as ſome ſtreſs ſeems to have been laid upon the precedents which you have cited, That, even ſuppoſing them to be more appoſite to the point than on examination they appear to be, the ground on which the interpoſition of parliament was called for was eſſentially different from that of the motion now in queſtion. The Chief Juſtices were amenable to no other juriſdiction; while the legality of the warrant, iſſued by Lord Halifax, was not only capable of being tried in the ordinary methods of proceeding, but actually put into a courſe of trial.

The case of Lord Marlborough was that of holding correspondence with rebels: And, in this, you yourself are willing to allow, I beg pardon, *connive at* the use of general warrants. The warrant issued in the case of Lord Danby, is far from resembling that which was issued by Lord Halifax. There was not, in Lord Danby, even the pretence of any crime; and, therefore, it is exactly of the same nature with those warrants which were granted, not by Lord Halifax, but by *Mr. Pitt.*

Had the proposed remedy been designed at the root of the evil, the resolution would have been worded so as to include a species of warrants; which, though not resulting from the case immediately under consideration, was by far more injurious to the liberty of the subject; warrants directing the apprehension of persons, without specifying the crimes for which they were to be taken up, and which the Secretary of State, who had issued them, did not attempt to defend upon any general principle.

But I return to the ſubject more immediately before us. And I ſubmit to you my reaſons for thinking, not only that the Minority did not avow their deſign, of confining themſelves to the warrant granted againſt Mr. Wilkes; but that you, who have had leiſure in your retirement to form for them this motive, and the diſtinction upon which it is founded, will not find it ſerviceable to your cauſe. For, having granted that it is juſtifiable to connive at the uſe of general warrants in the caſe of high-treaſon, in conſideration of the public danger, the nature of the offence, and the neceſſity of preventing its dangerous conſequences; it follows that, whereever theſe circumſtances are found, in that caſe a general warrant may be iſſued.

It remains only to aſk, Whether, in the caſe of Mr. Wilkes, theſe circumſtances did not concur? After what has been already obſerved, on this part of the ſubject, it is needleſs to inſiſt any further.

BUT with what propriety can you aſſert, that the caſe, upon which the propoſed reſolution was founded, was taken up by the Minority, entirely unconnected with Mr. Wilkes? I would juſt call to your recollection the ſubject of Mr. Wilkes's complaint, upon the firſt day of the ſeſſion, when the uſual courſe of proceedings was interrupted by his ſtarting from his ſeat; and, whilſt the Speaker was directing the clerk to read the cuſtomary bill, attempting to ſtate to the Houſe the breach of privilege which had been committed by the warrant iſſued againſt him. Was it the caſe alone that was taken up, when you, with many others, were of opinion that the uſual bill ſhould not be read, in order to give Mr. Wilkes the plauſible plea of having put the Houſe in poſſeſſion of his complaint? What was the language of the party, before the diſcuſſion of the point of privilege? That a moſt outragious inſult had been committed on a Member of the Legiſlature: That the liberty of the ſubject had been violated, in a moſt unparallelled manner; and that it was of the utmoſt conſequence to the preſervation

ſervation of freedom, that immediate reparation ſhould be made.

You will allow me to obſerve here, by the way, how unfortunate it was that the Houſe of Commons ſhould be the only place in which you did *not* think fit to give your reaſons for your opinion, that Mr. Wilkes was entitled to privilege. When, indeed, the *unhappy* man was adjudged to have no ſuch title, and every artificial delay had been attempted, which the moſt fertile imagination could invent, among which I would by no means forget the *medical* appeal to his bleeding wounds, thoſe *poor dumb mouths* which were to ſpeak ſo feelingly to compaſſion; when even a day's reſpite was thought worth obtaining; when ſucceſſive trials had been fruitleſsly made to procraſtinate the deciſion; then, and not till then, was the cauſe ſeparated from the man: Then ſtood forth two *candid* Gentlemen, who profeſſed to take up the matter upon Public Conſiderations. If that conduct can be called *candid*, which took every poſſible ſtep to procure that cenſure on Lord Halifax, which, in words, they were ſo forward to diſclaim: Yet, as if they were ſtill loth to abandon every thing that had a relation to the perſon of their champion, they ſuſpended even their eager deſires for the condemnation of the inſtruments employed by Government, till Mr. Wilkes's ſervant might be ſent for from Paris. What the depoſition of ſuch a man could avail, in a queſtion merely of public liberty, and in which every *perſonal* conſideration was pretended to be ſet aſide; I will leave it to thoſe Gentlemen to decide, whoſe firſt ſtep, in this great *national* cauſe, was the bringing on a complaint againſt *individuals*, and an attempt to delay their juſtification till they ſhould have rendered it impoſſible, (I mean conſiſtently with ſound concluſion) by voting the conduct, fortified as it was by a continued ſtream of precedents, to have been unwarrantable and illegal.

METHINKS the ſound of *Candour* ſtill grates upon my ear, reverberated by the parade of compliments which were ſo laviſhly beſtowed on the Gentlemen who affected to appear advocates in the cauſe of the Public; while, in truth, they were in the track which Mr. Wilkes's moſt devoted adherents could have wiſhed them to purſue. To what other end were the efforts, in the beginning of the winter's campaign, than the endeavouring to have the accuſation, which had been tricked up, examined in a manner to which neither the dignity of the Houſe, nor the ſituation of the accuſer entitled it?

AND, with regard to decency of language, no great merit, I truſt, will be aſſumed from their having ſpared opprobrious words againſt the Noble Earls, who were the objects of the reſolution. If this be indeed all the candour ſo much praiſed, I will not churliſhly refuſe to commend *two Baronets ſpeaking in a Houſe of Parliament, for not reviling two Secretaries of State, who had acted in ſtrict conformity with the eſtabliſhed cuſtom of their office.* And yet I would juſt remind you, that the deciſion of the queſtion upon privilege had taken the weapons from their hands. They could no longer pathetically deſcribe the inſolence of office, oppreſſing an injured Member of Parliament, and trampling upon the rights of the Commons of Great Britain; nor could their Lordſhips, in this ſituation, have been ſtiled the Noble Convicts.

Be the candour, however, of theſe Gentlemen what it may, the connection of the caſe taken up by the Minority, with the cauſe of Mr. Wilkes, is indiſputable from the ſimilarity of the methods purſued by Mr. Wilkes's defenders and by the advocates for the reſolution; from the eagerneſs with which it was preſſed by Mr. Wilkes's warmeſt friends, and from the numbers upon the diviſion.---The kingdom, you ſay, has been tried upon this topic, and the art has failed. As to the fact itſelf, if your own behaviour was ſuch as to diſclaim any connection with Mr. Wilkes, you have however no right to aſſert this of the reſt of the party.

You are not, and perhaps it is fortunate for the Miniſtry that you are not, the guide of their counſels, or the vehicle of their ſentiments. You know it is from other lips they take their tone. You are not involved in their indiscretions, but your conduct does not excuse theirs.

LET me, in addition to the proofs already offered, remind you of the declarations of those turbulent boys, the chosen and avowed oracles of the party, who professed themselves tied to Mr. Wilkes by the bands of friendship, and honoured by the tie. Recollect that we must attribute to this motive the factious Court which was formed in Great George-Street; for we cannot suppose those who formed it to have been indifferent to the cause of their Champion, and giving him support only because he had insulted the Crown and the Senate.

ANOTHER point which you propose to prove, is, That it was not an inconsistent conduct in those who appeared for the motion, to reject the remedy of a bill: And the reason you give for it is, That they could not vote for a bill to regulate what they did not admit to be legal. To which you have added the insinuation, that the Ministry were not, though they ought

to

to have been, earneſt in the ſupport of the bill.

BUT, Sir, has not your affection for the favourite antitheſis deceived you into the uſe of what was only the appearance of an argument? I do not know upon what foundation you aſſert that this word *regulate*, upon which the argument is grounded, was in the title of the bill? In *generals*, and in phyſics, the axiom is an undoubted one, that it is impoſſible to regulate what is not allowed to exiſt. But, apply this to the caſe before you, and you will ſee that the fallacy lies in the equivocal uſe of the word *regulate*. Take the queſtion out of *generals*, and it amounts to no more than this, Whether thoſe who aſſerted that theſe warrants were illegal, ſhould not have paſſed a bill forbidding the uſe of them?

THE Minority had aſſerted, each as they were able, but none of them with ſo much life and eloquence as Mr. Townſhend, that, upon the paſſing the reſolution propoſed, the eſſence of perſonal and private liberty depended.

They

They could not therefore, conſiſtently with thoſe aſſertions, refuſe: And, had they been ſincere in them, they would have gladly embraced the remedy of a bill, which was expreſsly offered to be drawn upon the plan, and in the words of their own motion. The Miniſtry thought *all* interpoſition of parliament unneceſſary, unwiſe, and dangerous. They were willing, however, to acquieſce in the only conſtitutional method of doing it. It could not therefore be expected, that they ſhould take upon themſelves to paſs a bill, which they thought the occaſion did not require. But it is difficult to conceive what reaſons could influence the Minority to depart from the object of their moſt vehement purſuit, when offered to be backed by an authority, which, taking the ſhape of a law, muſt have made the remedy more effectual. For one can hardly imagine, that what was circulated in the firſt peeviſhneſs of diſappointment, could have any real weight upon their minds; and that they could ſo far forget the duties of ſenators and of citizens, as to neglect what they had called eſſential to the ſecurity of the liberty

berty of the ſubject, merely becauſe the protection was adminiſtered through the channel of a gentleman, who was obnoxious to them as party-men.

BUT, whatever be the reaſons which operated, certain it is that a very extraordinary change took place in the conſtitution of the Minority, between the 17th and 21ſt of February. The heat of their political fever had ſubſided into a fit of the cold ague; and thoſe who on Friday declared themſelves unable to cloſe their eyes, till, by ſome reſolution of the Houſe, King's Meſſengers might be prevented from interrupting their ſlumbers, had fallen into ſo ſound and tranquil a ſleep, that the Tueſday morning paſſed away before they were ſufficiently awake to attend and ſupport a bill conceived in the words of that reſolution.

AFTER what had been ſaid on this ſubject, you go on to give the defenders of the Majority an objection, which ſeems principally to have been formed for the ſake of an anſwer intended to be given to it; and which, I think,

I think, I may venture to ſay, was never made, That the Minority proceeded by motion in the Houſe of Commons. Let us, however, examine your argument upon it. Your words are theſe: " Perhaps theſe Writers do not " know, that nothing is more uſual " or regular, in both Houſes of Parliament, than to take up important " matters of public adminiſtration ſeparately, in either Houſe; to expreſs " the ſenſe of that Houſe by a general reſolution; and, upon that reſolution, to bring in a bill."

No one will diſpute with you, that this method of proceeding is uſual and regular; but, if it was the intention of the Minority, in forming their reſolution, to carry it on to a bill, how could they, conſiſtently, refuſe a bill which was offered to be framed in the very words of the reſolution, for which they had ſo ineffectually contended?

For, though you have ſaid the Adminiſtration was *vanquiſhed in that day*, yet I cannot bring myſelf to think that it really was ſo, while I have before me ſo conſiderable a proof of your leisure, as the Defence of the Minority; and see, that, instead of setting the King's seal to an affectionate letter to the magnanimous King of Prussia, or remitting a subsidy to the King of Poland, you have had time to undertake that defence of the Two Hundred and Twenty, which it seems but *one* man in England would attempt.

I WILL not enquire of you, whether the fruits of this victory are yet seen in the stipulations which you have made for the introduction of your friends? But, give me leave to ask you, who, I doubt not, form your judgments upon something more substantial than words; Is the office, which, when the forts of government had been stormed, was to be your share of the plunder, now in your possession?

THE clamour of the song of triumph was indeed heard, and preparations were made to illuminate the Monument. The countenance and gestures of many had shewn all the marks of assured conquest; but, as long as there remains so much arithmetick in this kingdom, as to acknowledge that 234 is a larger number than 220, I ſhall have a right to ſay, That it was not the Adminiſtration, but the Minority, who were in that day vanquiſhed; *a Minority compoſed* (as it certainly was upon that day) *of men whoſe anceſtors, in their times, and of others, who in their own perſons, have ſigned the ſame warrants with thoſe iſſued by Lord Halifax, from the Revolution to this hour.*

I HAVE hitherto addreſſed myſelf to you by that title which you ſeem to affect, The Defender of the Minority; and yet, in the examination of your Defence, many ſubſtantial reaſons have concurred, in inducing me to think that you are not of their party. You have with them, as a party, no bond of connection, no common opinions; you do not claſs with them in principles, ſentiments, or abilities. There are among them men of worth and virtue. If, to ſome of theſe, you are united by the ties of friendſhip, to others by thoſe of eſteem, theſe bonds tie every generous mind, and in this ſenſe every honeſt man is of their party; and in no other are you of it. With the common run of ſecond-hand diſcarded politicians, which compoſe the Minority, you have no ſuch union: You are too wiſe and too delicate to become of their party; they are too ignorant and untractable, to become of yours. Their contemptible ignorance of true policy, their eaſy credulity, their viſionary ſchemes, their illiberal abuſe, are as far removed from your character, as your real knowledge, quick ſenſibility, and temperate oppoſition is from theirs.

In fact, Sir, the Oppoſition have never had any right to call you theirs. You parted from the Miniſtry upon a ſubject quite of a private and perſonal nature; upon a point which, however eſſential you might think it to your own intereſt and reputation, you could not, nor did you ever repreſent, as intereſting the Public. You had not, during the courſe of the laſt ſeſſion, ſentiments, upon the great meaſures of the year, different from thoſe of the King's ſervants. That this is true of the queſtions of Finance and Coloniſation, I have this proof: That, well-grounded as you are on theſe ſubjects, proceeding upon ſolid principles, and able to refer to them, and to illuſtrate by them all that particular information which you know ſo well how to obtain; and having, with theſe abilities, no want of inclination to oppoſe, you choſe to be abſent upon a ſubject in itſelf ſo complicated, upon proviſions in their operations neceſſarily ſo uncertain, when ſuch claſhing intereſts were to be attempered, the riches and ſtrength of our colonies cultivated, and their dependence ſecured; when a new world was to be ſubjected to fiſcal laws; that, upon ſuch a various and complex ſubject, you, ſo capable and ſo deſirous of ſhining, ſhould, contrary to your promiſe, be ſilent; ſhews that you approved the ſyſtem, and that your ingenuous mind would not ſuffer you to cavil at clauſes, when you approved the principles and purpoſes of the bill.

UPON the conteſt of Cyder, you cannot but remember what jealouſy and offence the Oppoſition received from your adherence to your own ſentiments, which were thoſe of the Miniſtry.

THERE

There remains, therefore, only the caſe of Mr. Wilkes, upon the firſt emergent point of which, that of privilege, I muſt ſuppoſe you to have been at leaſt half a convert to the ſide of Government. You ſurely, Sir, were ſtagger'd at leaſt by the weighty arguments of it's friends; for I muſt think that to no lighter motive you would have ſacrificed the labours of the ſummer and autumn, and the often-rehearſed eloquence of the winter. Upon the laſt point of it, the pamphlet before me is the ſtrongeſt proof that you are not only united with, but an advocate for the Miniſter. You have adopted his reaſonings and ſentiments, and I have only to congratulate the Miniſter upon ſo honourable an acceſſion to his party, and to admire the force of Truth upon a ſenſible mind; which thus compels you, perhaps imperceptibly to yourſelf, to range yourſelf on her ſide, though ſhe votes with the Majority. So little are you in concert with the Minority, that you have quitted the ground which they had taken as their moſt tenable poſt, and taken that which they, and even you, will find indefenſible.

THERE is only one part of the pamphlet of which I ſhall take the liberty of complaining to you, Sir; it is the concluſion. To prove in what an uncertain ſitutation *our moſt eſſential liberty, our undoubted birthright, ſtands, I beg pardon*, hangs *at this hour; it is aſſerted, that Lord Halifax may iſſue out another general warrant, upon the pretence of the laſt libel, the Budget.* This conveys an inſinuation, though I will not think you meant one, that there was nothing in the ſeditious libel, the North Briton, but what is equally to be found in this laſt pamphlet; and yet, Sir, you think that the former *traduced the honour of the Crown, and injured the dignity of Parliament.* It inſinuates, that puniſhment was inflicted on the former Writer, for his oppoſition to the Miniſtry, and that the ſame principles ſubject Sir G. S. to the ſame proſecution. Theſe inſinuations are more worthy of your cauſe than of your character.

THE Miniſter in the Houſe of Commons ſeems to have been long enough verſed in political life, to pay chearfully that tax to ſlander which is ſo conſtantly levelled upon every honeſt man

man who ſerves his country. He has ſhewn that he thought the ſevereſt puniſhment due to the former, for his treaſonable writings; to the latter, you ſay, he has not even condeſcended to direct a reply. You have no right therefore to uſe words, which inſinuate that he thinks alike on theſe two papers; and that he reſents equally an attack upon himſelf and an inſult upon his Sovereign. What his ſentiments may be upon the Budget, it is not, I ſuppoſe, eaſy to know. For my own part, I cannot poſſibly figure to myſelf a Miniſter ſo ſore, as to be hurt by that pamphlet: But I can eaſily imagine, that there are other reaſons for leaving it unanſwered, beſides the thinking it unanſwerable.

And now, Sir, you will decide whether, in the Defence of the Minority, you have ſtated the legal and parliamentary tranſactions with preciſion: Whether you have aſſigned the true motives of the conduct of your friends, or even ſuch as they will avow: Whether you have vindicated their paſt oppoſition, or given them good grounds for their continuing in it the next ſeſſions:

ſions: And whether you have proved the neceſſity, or propriety, of their having contended, and continuing to move for parliamentary interpoſition, in a caſe which is in a courſe of legal determination, and *ſub judice*, with reſpect to the Courts of Appeal, and which, in the Court of Common Pleas, has been actually determined.

FINIS.

www.ingramcontent.com/pod-product-compliance
Lightning Source LLC
Chambersburg PA
CBHW021441090426
42739CB00009B/1579

* 9 7 8 3 3 3 7 1 9 5 8 0 9 *